101 Margaritas

KIM HAASARUD

Photography by
Alexandra Grablewski

JOHN WILEY & SONS, INC.

Text Copyright © 2006 by Kim Haasarud. All rights reserved.
Photography Copyright © 2006 by Alexandra Grablewski.

Published by John Wiley & Sons, Inc., Hoboken, New Jersey.
Published simultaneously in Canada.

For general information about our other products and services, please contact our Customer Care Department within the United States at (800) 762-2974, outside the United States at (317) 572-3993 or fax (317) 572-4002.

Wiley also publishes its books in a variety of electronic formats. Some content that appears in print may not be available in electronic books. For more information about Wiley prod-ucts, visit our web site at www.wiley.com

Food styling by Jee Levin.
Prop styling by Leslie Siegel.
Design by Elizabeth Van Itallie

Facing title page: Blueberry Margarita, recipe no. 64.

Library of Congress Cataloging-in-Publication Data:

Haasarud, Kim.
  101 margaritas / Kim Haasarud ; photography by Alexandra Grablewski.
    p. cm.
  Includes index.
  ISBN-13: 978-0-7645-9986-6 (cloth)
  ISBN-10: 0-7645-9986-0 (cloth)
  1. Margaritas. 2. Tequila. 3. Cocktails. I. Title.
  TX951.H2 2006
  641.8'74--dc22
                                        2005009863
Printed in China

10 9 8 7 6 5 4 3 2 1

TO MY HUSBAND, KEVIN.

The best taste-tester around.
Thanks for all your support and encouragement.

The Margarita

The story goes that the Margarita was created by a woman named Margarita Sames. She mixed her favorite liqueur, Cointreau, with tequila and lime juice and served it in glasses dusted with salt. Another theory is that it was named after Margarete, a descendent of the Spanish explorer Ponce de León. My favorite is the story of the Greek god Agavethenos, whose fiery spirit could only be tamed by the soothing goddess of citrus Margarthena, hence the Margarita. . . . Okay, I made that last one up, but the point is no one really knows where or when the Margarita was created, only that its centerpiece ingredients is tequila, accented with orange liqueur and lime juice.

Today, the Margarita can be found in nearly every bar and restaurant in the Western Hemisphere, and with the increasingly widespread popularity of tequilas, it is possible to find the Margarita throughout Europe and across Asia and the Pacific Rim. The Margarita, *the* happy hour staple, has been known to fuel social gatherings and even to serve as a catalyst for life-changing decisions. (One year, my husband's family drank a pitcher of Margaritas and then decided to move to Switzerland.)

In the past, the tequilas that were commonly available in the United States were lower-quality blends. Lime and salt were necessary to tame their harshness. Today's super-premium 100 percent blue agave tequilas are akin to New World cognacs, and are referred to by a nouveau breed of connoisseur as "sipping tequilas." These recently introduced tequilas have moved the benchmark of quality, and they range widely not only in aging methods and color, but also in taste. A great Margarita enhances—and does not mask—the essence of these tequilas.

MY MARGARITA PHILOSOPHY

Traditionally a Margarita is made with tequila, orange liqueur, lime juice, and sugar. It sounds simple enough, yet we've all had bad ones . . . too bitter, too sour, too sweet, watered down, too strong, too weak, or just tasting like it's missing something. The key to making the perfect Margarita is balance. A balance of sweet and sour notes with the right amount of tequila is what makes a *good* Margarita great.

Understanding that creating a Margarita is a balancing act and not the result of using a specific ingredient opens up a new world of flavors not traditionally associated with the Margarita. Coffee, ginger, sake, rhubarb, and hazelnut are just a few examples of how the cocktails in this book take the Margarita to a new level. While the traditional favorites (classic, strawberry, passionfruit, raspberry, etc.) are all here, this book breaks the Margarita boundaries to include some wild and unique recipes that hopefully will both entice and surprise you.

INGREDIENTS

I strongly recommend using fresh, high-quality ingredients. While they may be a little more expensive, they make a dramatic difference in flavor. For example, when using real, freshly squeezed lime juice with 100% blue agave tequila, the lime juice enhances the finer subtleties in the tequila. On the other hand, using lime juice with a lower-quality tequila usually serves only to mask the harsh and bitter flavors of inferior tequilas. There is no excuse for a bitter aftertaste when with a little effort and creativity you can add accents that make the subtle *terroir* of the agave explode.

SALT VS. NO SALT

Salt for many people is synonymous with the Margarita. Its original purpose was to act as a counterbalance to the fieriness of some tequilas, while accenting the sweet-and-sour flavor. Many 100 percent blue agave tequilas already have a subtle saline flavor to them. These days, with superior blue agave tequilas widely available, salt is no longer needed. But as a remnant of tradition, the use of salt has become customary. While it is a popular addition to the Margarita, it can also be disastrous. For most fruit-based Margaritas, I would recommend a coarse sugar rim or no rim at all. Throughout the book, I've clearly indicated how best to serve each recipe. The salt shaker icon with the red checkmark shows that a salted rim is appropriate, and the salt shaker with the "X" through it accompanies those recipes that should not be served with salt. My personal preference is not to use salt; it distracts from the subtle nature of premium agave tequilas. That said, if using a standard tequila, feel free to use salt, but please do so with discretion. For a standard salt rim, wet the rim of the Margarita glass with lime juice. Rose's Lime Juice works best—it is a little thicker and stickier than regular lime juice. Dip the wet rim into coarse salt several times to ensure coverage and set aside.

SIMPLE SYRUP

Sugar is a key ingredient in a Margarita, whether it's in the form of a sweet spirit, fruit, or simple syrup. It is one of the key performers in the balancing act. Often, when you've had a Margarita that is too sour or too bitter, it is the *balance of sugar* that is off. Simple syrup is the most basic form of sugar that is used in Margaritas. If you plan on making some Margaritas (or just about any other cocktail) for company, prepare a batch of this simple syrup in advance. You can store it in the refrigerator, covered, for up to 5 days.

$\frac{1}{2}$ **cup white sugar**
$\frac{1}{2}$ **cup hot water**

In a small bowl or glass, combine the sugar and hot water and stir until completely dissolved. Let cool completely before using.

Agave nectar is another form of sugar that can be used in lieu of simple syrup. It is extracted from the agave plant itself and is sweeter than refined sugar. It also doesn't have the same "sugar rush" effect. It is excellent in Margaritas, and although it may be difficult to find in your local supermarket, it's worth the extra effort. You can find it at www.agavenectar.com.

Fire and water, sweet and sour . . . this is the balancing act that goes into the perfect Margarita. Whether you're having a rowdy round with friends or a quiet sipping experience with a loved one, the Margarita in all its manifestations is a drink for the ages. I encourage you to try one . . . and experiment with the wide range of fresh ingredients and premium agave tequilas that will lead to an extraordinary Margarita experience. Cheers!

—KIM HAASARUD, THE LIQUID CHEF

Classic MARGARITA

2 ounces tequila
2 ounces simple syrup (see page 9)
1 ounce Cointreau
1 ounce lime juice
1 ounce lemon juice
lime wheel, for garnish

Combine the ingredients in a cocktail shaker filled with ¾ cup cubed ice and shake vigorously. Pour with the ice or strain into a glass, depending on personal preference. If serving frozen, combine the ingredients in a blender with ¾ cup crushed ice, blend until smooth, and pour into a glass. Garnish with a lime wheel.

Grand Gold MARGARITA

2 ounces tequila
2 ounces simple syrup (see page 9)
1 ounce Grand Marnier
1 ounce lime juice
1 ounce lemon juice
lime wedge or wheel, for garnish

Combine the ingredients in a cocktail shaker filled with ice and shake vigorously. Strain into a glass. If serving frozen, combine the ingredients in a blender with ¾ cup crushed ice and blend until smooth. Pour into a glass. Garnish with a lime wedge.

Añejo MARGARITA

For this variation, substitute an añejo tequila for the regular tequila, 1 ounce Damiana (a sweet herbal Mexican liqueur) for the Grand Marnier, and add a splash of orange juice.

Platinum MARGARITA

2 ounces gold tequila
1½ ounces agave nectar (or simple syrup, see page 9)
1 ounce lime juice
1 ounce lemon juice
½ ounce Cointreau
½ ounce Grand Marnier
splash of orange juice
lime wedge, for garnish

Combine the ingredients in a cocktail shaker filled with ice and shake vigorously. Strain into a glass. If serving frozen, combine the ingredients in a blender with ¾ cup crushed ice and blend until smooth. Pour into a glass. Garnish with a lime wedge.

Low-Carb MARG

This margarita was created by renowned mixologist Dale DeGroff, author of *The Craft of the Cocktail*.

- **2 ounces Gran Centenario Plata Tequila**
- **¾ ounce lime juice**
- **3 drops orange extract (available in the spice aisle of the supermarket)**
- **1 packet Splenda, dissolved in 2 tablespoons water**
- **1 piece orange peel (1 x 2 inches)**

Combine the tequila, lime juice, orange extract, and dissolved Splenda in a cocktail shaker with ice. Squeeze the orange peel into the shaker and shake for a good 10 seconds. Strain into a glass.

Chambord

2 ounces tequila
1 ounce Chambord
1 ounce simple syrup (see page 9)
½ ounce lemon juice
½ ounce lime juice
lime wedge, for garnish

Combine the ingredients in a cocktail shaker filled with ice and
shake vigorously. Strain into a glass. If serving frozen, combine
the ingredients in a blender with ¾ cup ice and blend until
smooth. Pour into a glass. Garnish with a lime wedge.

6

Blue MARGARITA

2 ounces tequila
1 ounce blue curaçao
1 ounce simple syrup (see page 9)
½ ounce lime juice
½ ounce lemon juice

Combine the ingredients in a cocktail shaker filled with ¾ cup ice and shake vigorously. Pour into a glass. If serving frozen, combine the ingredients in a blender with ¾ cup ice and blend until smooth. Pour into a glass.

Margatini

2 ounces Herradura Añejo or Silver tequila
1 ounce Cointreau
1 ounce simple syrup (see page 9)
½ ounce lemon juice
½ ounce lime juice
lime wheel, for garnish

Combine the ingredients in a cocktail shaker filled with ice and shake vigorously. Strain into a glass. Garnish with a lime wheel.

Lemon-Basil

MARGARITA

A great cocktail to serve at brunches, bridal showers, and spring and summer cocktail parties.

> ½ lemon, seeded and thinly sliced into half wheels
> 2 basil leaves
> ½ ounce simple syrup (see page 9)
> 2 ounces gold tequila
> 1 ounce Grand Marnier

Mash together the lemon slices, basil leaves, and simple syrup in a glass with the end of a spoon, just enough for the ingredients to mix together. Add the tequila, Grand Marnier, and ¾ cup crushed ice and stir until completely mixed.

9

Meyer Lemon
MARGARITA

Meyer lemons are much sweeter and more delicate in flavor than the Eureka lemons most commonly found in supermarkets.

> 1½ ounces tequila
> 1 ounce Cointreau
> 1 ounce Meyer lemon juice (the juice of about ½ Meyer lemon)
> ¾ ounce simple syrup (see page 9)
> lemon rind, for garnish

Combine the ingredients in a cocktail shaker filled with ¾ cup ice and shake vigorously. Pour into a glass and add a strip of lemon rind for garnish.

Bitter Lemon
MARGARITA

For a slightly more bitter Margarita, add 1 to 2 ounces Schweppes bitter lemon and serve over ice.

Grapefruit MARGARITA

If you can find them, pummelos make the best Grapefruit Margaritas. They are very aromatic and have just the right balance of sweet and sour. They can be found at some farmer's markets. Salting the rim is optional.

2 ounces tequila
2 ounces freshly squeezed grapefruit juice
1 ounce Cointreau
½ ounce lemon juice
½ grapefruit slice, for garnish

Combine the ingredients in a cocktail shaker filled with ice and shake vigorously. Strain into a glass. If serving frozen, combine the ingredients in a blender with ¾ cup ice and blend until smooth. Pour into a glass. Garnish with a half grapefruit slice.

Mojita Rita

An agave spin on the classic cocktail, the Mojito.

¾ lime, cut into quarters
5 to 6 mint leaves
1 teaspoon light brown sugar
½ ounce water
1½ ounces tequila
1 ounce Cointreau

Mash together the lime quarters, mint leaves, brown sugar, and water in a glass until the mint leaves start to bruise; this releases the oils and aromas in the mint. Add the tequila, Cointreau, and ¾ cup crushed ice to the glass. Stir very well (don't shake), bringing the mint leaves to the top of the drink and dissolving all the sugar. Serve immediately.

Pink Lemonade
MARGARITA

2 ounces tequila
1 ounce triple sec
2 tablespoons pink lemonade frozen concentrate
1 ounce 7-Up
lemon wheel, for garnish

Combine the tequila, triple sec, and pink lemonade concentrate in a cocktail shaker with ¾ cup ice and shake vigorously, enough to break up the frozen concentrate. Pour into a glass. Top off with 7-Up and garnish with a lemon wheel.

Limeade MARGARITA

Use the same recipe as above, but substitute limeade frozen concentrate for the pink lemonade. You can also serve this one frozen, without the 7-Up. Garnish with a lime wedge.

Cosmo Rita

A margarita twist on the popular Cosmopolitan.

> 1 ounce tequila
> 1 ounce cranberry juice
> ¾ ounce orange-flavored vodka
> ¾ ounce Cointreau
> ½ ounce lime juice
> ½ ounce simple syrup (see page 9)
> orange peel twist, for garnish

Combine the ingredients in a cocktail shaker filled with ice. Shake vigorously and strain into a glass. If serving frozen, combine the ingredients in a blender with ¾ cup ice and blend briefly until smooth. Pour into a glass. Garnish with an orange peel twist.

16

Key Lime MARGARITA

1 ½ ounces tequila
1 ½ ounces McGillicuddy's vanilla schnapps
½ ounce key lime juice (available in specialty supermarkets)
½ ounce simple syrup ((see page 9)
4 tablespoons vanilla sugar (optional), for garnish

Combine the ingredients in a cocktail shaker filled with ice and shake vigorously. Strain into a glass. If serving frozen, combine the ingredients in a blender with ¾ cup ice and blend until smooth. Pour into a glass. For a more vivid green key lime, add a touch of Midori (melon liqueur). Instead of salt, try coating the rim of the glass with vanilla sugar.

To make vanilla sugar, combine 1 teaspoon vanilla extract and 4 tablespoons white sugar.

Lemon Meringue
MARGARITA

A great after-dinner cocktail.

1½ ounces gold tequila
1 ounce Cointreau
1 ounce lemon juice
1 ounce simple syrup (see page 9)
1 large egg white
powdered sugar (optional), for garnish

Combine the ingredients in a cocktail shaker with ¾ cup ice and shake vigorously. Pour into a rimmed glass or strain into a cognac glass. There should be a layer of foam on top. For a powdered sugar rim, coat the edge of the cocktail glass in simple syrup. Dip into powdered sugar several times to ensure coverage.

White MARGARITA

2 ounces white tequila
1 ounce triple sec
½ ounce lemon juice
1 scoop of lemon sorbet (soft)
grated zest of 1 lemon
lemon twist, for garnish

Combine the tequila, triple sec, lemon juice, sorbet, and zest in a blender with ½ cup ice and blend until smooth. Pour into a glass. Garnish with a lemon twist.

19

Limoncello

2 ounces gold tequila
1 ounce Limoncello
1 ounce simple syrup (see page 9)
½ ounce lemon juice
½ ounce lime juice
4 tablespoons lemon zest sugar (optional), for garnish

Combine the ingredients in a blender with ¾ cup crushed ice and blend until smooth. Pour into a glass. Try coating the rim of the glass with lemon zest sugar.

To make lemon zest sugar, combine zest of 1 lemon and 4 tablespoons coarse white sugar.

Blood Orange

2 ounces blood orange juice (the juice of ½ blood orange)
1½ ounces tequila
1 ounce triple sec
½ ounce simple syrup (see page 9)
splash of lime juice
blood orange wedge, for garnish

Combine the ingredients in a cocktail shaker filled with ice and shake vigorously. Strain into a glass. If serving frozen, combine the ingredients with ¾ cup crushed ice in a blender and blend until smooth. Pour into a glass. Garnish with a blood orange wedge.

Disaronno MARGARITA

If you like the flavor of sweetened almonds, you'll love this one. Disaronno is an Italian amaretto liqueur. It is much sweeter than triple sec, so only half an ounce is needed. This recipe was taken from *The Joy of Mixology* by master mixologist Gary Regan.

1½ ounces white tequila
½ ounce Amaretto Disaronno
½ ounce lime juice

Combine the ingredients in a cocktail shaker filled with ice and shake vigorously. Strain into a chilled glass.

22

Orange Delight
MARGARITA

2 ounces tequila
1 ounce triple sec
1 ounce orange juice
1 scoop orange sorbet (or sherbet)
2 ounces orange soda (e.g., Orange Crush, Sunkist)
orange slice, for garnish

Combine the tequila, triple sec, orange juice, and orange sorbet in a blender with ½ cup ice and blend until smooth. Pour into a glass. Top off with orange soda. Garnish with orange slice.

Orange Mint MARGARITA

For a frostier version, skip the orange soda and blend with just the orange sorbet. Throw in 6 to 7 mint leaves for a hint of coolness.

Strawberry MARGARITA

2 ounces tequila
1 ounce triple sec
½ ounce lime juice
¼ cup sliced strawberries sprinkled with 1 tablespoon
   white sugar
1 whole strawberry, for garnish
coarse sugar, for garnish

Combine the ingredients in a blender with ¾ cup ice and blend until smooth. Pour into a glass. Garnish with a whole strawberry (with the stem). For a sugar rim, wet the rim of a glass with lime juice then dip into coarse sugar. Dip several times to ensure coverage.

Strawberry Banana MARGARITA

Add ½ banana, ¾ ounce triple sec, and ½ ounce banana liqueur for a creamier banana version.

Fruit Cocktail

MARGARITA

While I am a huge proponent of using the freshest ingredients, this is an easy Margarita to make with canned fruit cocktail, which is readily available any time of year. The juices in the fruit cocktail serve as a sweet counterbalance to the tequila.

$1\frac{1}{2}$ ounces white tequila
1 ounce triple sec
$\frac{1}{2}$ cup canned fruit cocktail (with the juice)
2 ounces orange juice

Combine the ingredients in a blender with ¾ cup ice and blend until smooth. Pour into a glass. Garnish with a few pieces of the fruit cocktail, speared on a toothpick.

Banana MARGARITA

2 ounces tequila
1½ ounces banana schnapps
½ ounce light cream
½ banana
simple syrup (optional)
banana chips, for garnish

Combine tequila, banana schnapps, light cream, and banana in a blender with ½ cup ice and blend until smooth. Add simple syrup to taste if you prefer your Margarita sweeter. Pour into a glass and garnish with banana chips.

Strorange MARGARITA

29

1½ ounces white tequila
1 ounce Grand Marnier
1 ounce orange juice
½ ounce lime juice
½ ounce lemon juice
½ ounce simple syrup (see page 9)
2 strawberries, stem removed
strawberry and/or orange wedge, for garnish
4 tablespoons orange zest sugar (optional), for garnish

Combine the ingredients in a blender with ¾ cup ice and blend until smooth. Pour into a glass and garnish with the wedges of strawberry and orange. For an orange sugar rim, mix 4 tablespoons coarse white sugar with the grated zest of 1 orange.

Sunrise MARGARITA

2 ounces tequila
4 ounces orange juice
1 ounce triple sec
splash of lemon juice
$\frac{1}{2}$ ounce grenadine
cherry, for garnish

Combine the tequila, orange juice, triple sec, and lemon juice in a cocktail shaker filled with ice and shake vigorously. Strain into a glass. Add the grenadine, which will settle at the bottom of the glass, and garnish with a cherry.

Daiquirita

1 ounce white rum
1 ounce simple syrup (see page 9)
¾ ounce white tequila
¾ ounce triple sec
½ ounce lemon juice
½ ounce lime juice
lime twist, for garnish

Combine the ingredients in a cocktail shaker filled with ¾ cup ice and shake vigorously. Pour into a glass. If serving frozen, combine the ingredients in a blender with ¾ cup crushed ice and blend until smooth. Pour into a glass. You can coat the rim of the glass in a sugar-salt mixture. Garnish with a lime twist.

Strawberry Daiquirita

Add ¼ cup sweetened strawberries to the recipe above for a frosty, berry version, which must be served frozen. Garnish with a half or whole strawberry.

Passionfruit MARGARITA

2 ounces white tequila
1 ounce Alize Wild Passion liqueur
1 ounce passionfruit puree (available at specialty supermarkets)
½ ounce lemon juice
½ ounce simple syrup (see page 9)
lemon wedge or wheel, for garnish

Combine the ingredients in a blender with ¾ cup crushed ice and
blend until smooth. Pour into a glass. Garnish with a lemon
wedge or wheel. The Passionfruit Margarita can also be made
without the puree, if you are unable to find it. However, the puree
does add a more robust flavor to the Margarita.

Berry Passionate MARGARITA

Add ¼ cup sweetened strawberries and raspberries to the above
recipe for an ultrapassionate frozen Margarita. Top off with a few
raspberries as a garnish.

Brunch

¾ ounce orange juice
¾ ounce pink lemonade
¾ ounce pineapple juice
½ ounce tequila
½ ounce triple sec
2 ounces champagne (or sparkling wine)
orange, pineapple or lemon wedge, for garnish

Combine the orange juice, pink lemonade, pineapple juice,
tequila, and triple sec in a cocktail shaker filled with ice and
shake vigorously. Strain into a glass and top off with the champagne. Garnish with fruit.

Kumquat MARGARITA

2 ounces gold tequila
1 ounce Grand Marnier
1 ounce simple syrup (see page 9)
2 to 3 seeded kumquats (sweet)
splash of lemon juice

Combine the ingredients in a blender with ½ cup ice and blend
until smooth. Pour into a glass.

36

Cherimoya MARGARITA

Cherimoya is a fruit originating in South America. Its custard-like flesh lends itself to wonderful, creamy cocktails and desserts. While you may not be able to find cherimoyas at your local grocery store, they can be found at many produce and farmer's markets.

> ½ ripe cherimoya
> 1½ ounces tequila
> 1½ ounces Damiana liqueur (a sweet, herbal Mexican liqueur)
> ½ ounce light cream (or half-and-half)
> grated nutmeg (optional), for garnish

Spoon out the custardlike cherimoya flesh, discarding the seeds, and place in a blender. Add the tequila, Damiana, cream, and ½ cup ice and blend until smooth. Pour into a glass. Top with a sprinkle of nutmeg, if desired.

Plum MARGARITA

2 ounces tequila
1 ounce Cointreau
½ ounce orange juice
½ plum (not peeled)
splash of lemon juice

Combine the ingredients in a blender with ½ cup ice and blend
until smooth. Pour into a glass. If desired, coat the rim with a
mixture of sugar and salt.

Aphrodisiac

- 1 ounce white tequila
- 1 ounce B & B liqueur
- ¼ cup of mixed berries (e.g., strawberries, raspberries, blueberries, etc.)
- ¼ ripe fig, peeled

Combine the ingredients in a blender with ¾ cup ice and blend until smooth. Pour into a glass. An alternative to using the blender is to mash together the mixed berries and fig with the tequila and B & B with a spoon. Add ice and shake vigorously in a cocktail shaker. Strain, loosely, into a glass, letting pieces of fruit fall into the cocktail. Garnish with whole berries.

39

Pineapple MARGARITA

2 ounces pineapple juice (freshly squeezed or name brand)
1½ ounces tequila
1 ounce Cointreau
½ cup ripe crushed pineapple (best if fresh, not canned)
splash of lemon juice
splash of simple syrup (see page 9)
pineapple chunks, for garnish

Combine the ingredients in a blender with ½ cup ice and blend until smooth. Pour into a glass. Garnish with a pineapple chunks.

Pine–Orange–Banana MARGARITA

For a fruity, frosty, banana-flavored version, add the following: ¾ ounce pineapple juice, ¾ ounce orange juice, ½ ounce banana liqueur, and ½ banana.

Pomegranate MARGARITA

2 ounces tequila
2 ounces pomegranate juice
1 ounce triple sec
½ ounce lime juice
½ ounce simple syrup (see page 9)

Combine the ingredients in a cocktail shaker filled with ¾ cup ice and shake vigorously. Pour into a glass.

Rose MARGARITA

This variation of the pomegranate Margarita, made with tequila infused with pomegranate seeds, was created by Tony Abou-Ganim, founder of *The Modern Mixologist*.

1½ ounces Patrón Reposado infused with pomegranate seeds
¾ ounce Grand Marnier
juice of 1 small lime
2 ounces fresh lemon sour (2 parts lemon juice, 1 part simple syrup)

To infuse the tequila, cover 2 cups of pomegranate seeds with 1 bottle of Patrón Reposado and let sit for 1 month in a cool, dark place. To make the cocktail, combine the ingredients in a cocktail shaker with ¾ cup ice and shake well. Pour into a glass and garnish with pomegranate seeds.

(The juice is extracted from the seeds, but the seeds themselves are inedible.)

Cherry MARGARITA 44

1½ ounces white tequila
1 ounce triple sec
1 ounce simple syrup (see page 9)
1 ounce pomegranate juice
½ ounce lime juice
4 to 5 pitted fresh cherries (not maraschino), plus extra for
  garnish

Combine the ingredients in a blender with ¾ cup ice and blend
until smooth. Add pomegranate juice as needed to obtain smooth
consistency. Pour into a frozen Margarita glass. Garnish with a
stemmed cherry.

Cranberry MARGARITA

If you are unable to find presweetened cranberries at your local supermarket, you can combine ¼ cup whole cranberries with 3 tablespoons simple syrup in a pan over low heat. Cook, stirring frequently, until the berries become soft.

1½ ounces white tequila
1 ounce triple sec
¼ cup sweetened cranberries with juices
splash of lemon juice
white cranberry juice (optional)

Combine the ingredients in a blender with ¾ cup ice and blend until smooth, adding a bit of white cranberry juice, if desired, for a smoother consistency. There should be lots of little red cranberry flecks throughout the drink.

Berries Jubilee

MARGARITA

½ cup assorted seasonal berries (e.g., strawberries, blueberries,
  raspberries, etc.), cut in half if larger than ½ inch
¼ cup Grand Marnier
1½ ounces gold tequila
2 ounces simple syrup (see page 9)
splash of lemon juice
coarse sugar (optional), for garnish

Marinate the berries in the Grand Marnier for at least 1 hour.
Combine the berries, including the liquid, with the remaining
ingredients in a blender with ¾ cup ice and blend until smooth.
Pour into a glass. Coat the rim of the glass with coarse sugar, if
desired.

46

Coco-Pina MARGARITA

3 ounces pineapple juice
1½ ounces coconut rum
1 ounce tequila
¾ ounce sweetened coconut cream (e.g., Coco Lopez)
2 tablespoons pineapple chunks (optional)
pineapple wedge, for garnish

Combine the ingredients in a blender with about 1 cup ice and blend until smooth. Pour into a glass. Garnish with a pineapple wedge.

Coconut MARGARITA

1½ ounces coconut rum
1 ounce tequila
1 ounce coconut milk (found in the Thai section of most markets)
¾ ounce sweetened coconut cream (e.g., Coco Lopez)
toasted coconut shavings (optional), for garnish

Combine the ingredients in a blender with about 1 cup ice and blend until smooth. Pour into a glass.

48

Apple MARGARITA

2 ounces apple juice (preferably freshly pressed)
1½ ounces tequila
1 ounce Berentzen Apfel Korn (apple schnapps)
splash of lemon juice
¼ peeled apple (if serving frozen)
apple wedge (red or green), for garnish

Combine the ingredients in a cocktail shaker filled with ice and shake vigorously. Strain into a glass. If serving frozen, combine the ingredients (including the peeled apple) in a blender with ½ cup ice and blend until smooth. Pour into a glass. Garnish with an apple wedge.

49

Watermelon MARGARITA

1½ ounces tequila
1½ ounces watermelon schnapps
1 ounce simple syrup (see page 9)
½ ounce lemon juice
½ ounce lime juice
¼ cup of seeded watermelon flesh (if serving frozen)
watermelon rind, for garnish

Combine the ingredients in a cocktail shaker filled with ice and
shake vigorously. Strain into a glass. If serving frozen, combine
the ingredients including the watermelon flesh in a blender with
¾ cup ice and blend until smooth. Pour into a glass. Garnish with
small wedge of watermelon rind. If serving frozen, garnish with 3
to 4 watermelon seeds.

Mango MARGARITA

51

2 ounces tequila
1 ounce Cointreau
1 ounce orange juice
¼ mango slice (peeled)
1 scoop mango sorbet
mango slice, for garnish

Combine the ingredients in a blender with ¾ cup ice and blend until smooth. Pour into a glass. Garnish with a mango slice.

Midori MARGARITA

Midori is a bright green melon liqueur and is a popular ingredient
in many margaritas served in restaurants.

1½ ounces tequila
1½ ounces Midori
1 ounce simple syrup (see page 9)
½ ounce lime juice
½ ounce lemon juice

Combine the ingredients in a cocktail shaker filled with ¾ cup ice
and shake vigorously. Pour into a glass. If serving frozen, combine
the ingredients in a blender with ¾ cup crushed ice and blend
until smooth. Pour into a glass.

Cantaloupe MARGARITA

2 ounces tequila
1 ounce triple sec
1 ounce simple syrup (see page 9)
½ ounce Midori
½ ounce lemon juice
½ cup of cubed cantaloupe
cantaloupe balls, for garnish

Combine the ingredients in a blender with ¾ cup ice and blend until smooth. Pour into a glass. Garnish with a speared ball of cantaloupe.

Melon MARGARITA INFUSION

For a more intense version of the above recipe, try using a melon-infused tequila. Ball an entire cantaloupe (or honeydew, Crenshaw, etc., for added color and more complex flavors). Fill a large jar with melon balls, and then with tequila. Cover and infuse at room temperature overnight. Use in the recipe above, or serve the infused tequila over ice.

Rhubarb MARGARITA

One stalk of sweetened, cooked rhubarb is enough to make four margaritas, so invite some friends over when you try this one.

  1 stalk rhubarb, chopped
  ½ cup simple syrup (see page 9)
  1½ ounces white tequila
  1 ounce Grand Marnier
  basil leaf or mint leaf, for garnish

Cook the rhubarb stalk with the simple syrup in a pan over low heat until softened, about 5 minutes. Combine about ¼ of the rhubarb stalk and juices in a blender with the tequila, Grand Marnier, and ¾ cup ice and blend until smooth. Pour into a glass and garnish with a basil or mint leaf.

55

Prickly Pear
MARGARITA

Prickly pear juice can be difficult to find outside the southwestern United States, where the prickly pear is most commonly grown. It can also be a little expensive, since each fruit yields only a small amount of juice. Still, it's a Southwest favorite.

2 ounces tequila
¾ ounce Cointreau
½ ounce prickly pear juice
½ ounce lime juice

Combine the ingredients in a cocktail shaker filled with ice and shake vigorously. Strain into a glass. If serving frozen, combine ingredients in a blender with ¾ cup crushed ice and blend until smooth. Pour into a glass.

Frosty Nectarine
MARGARITA

2 ounces tequila
1 ounce Cointreau
½ nectarine, peeled and sliced
¼ cup peach sorbet
splash of half-and-half (optional)

Combine the ingredients in a blender with ¼ cup ice and blend until smooth. For a creamier texture, add a splash of half-and-half during the blending process. Garnish with a slice of nectarine.

Kiwi MARGARITA

2 ounces tequila
2 ounces pineapple juice
1 ounce triple sec
½ ounce lime juice
½ ounce simple syrup (see page 9)
1 kiwi fruit, peeled and quartered
half kiwi slice, for garnish
coarse sugar (optional), for garnish

Combine the ingredients in a blender with ½ cup ice and blend until smooth. Pour into a glass and garnish with a half kiwi slice. If desired, coat the rim of the glass with sugar.

58

Peach MARGARITA 59

2 ounces peach schnapps
1½ ounces white tequila
1 ounce orange juice
½ ounce Grand Marnier
½ ounce simple syrup (see page 9)
½ fresh peach, cut into quarters
splash of lemon juice
coarse sugar (optional), for garnish

Combine the ingredients in a blender with ¾ cup ice and blend until smooth. Pour into a glass. Coat the rim of the glass with sugar, if desired.

Fuzzy MARGARITA

Inspired by the populare cocktail, the Fuzzy Navel. Reduce the peach schnapps to 1 ounce, increase the orange juice to 2 ounces, increase the lemon juice to ½ ounce, and omit the Grand Marnier, simple syrup, and ½ peach. Combine in a cocktail shaker with ¾ cup ice, shake vigorously, and pour into a glass.

60

Peaches-n-Cream
MARGARITA

1½ ounces vanilla schnapps
1 ounce tequila
1 ounce light cream (or half-and-half)
1 scoop peach sorbet
¼ cup chopped fresh mango or peach

Combine the ingredients in a blender with ½ cup ice and blend until smooth. Pour into a glass.

61

Apricot MARGARITA 62

½ cup peeled and chopped ripe apricot
1 tablespoon sugar
2 ounces white tequila
1 ounce apricot brandy (or crème de noya if you can find it)
¼ ounce lemon juice
basil leaf, for garnish

Sprinkle the apricot with the sugar and let it sit for 15 minutes to absorb the sugar. Combine the sweetened apricots (with their juices) and remaining ingredients in a blender with ¾ cup ice and blend until smooth. Pour into a glass. Garnish with a basil leaf.

Raspberry MARGARITA

6 to 7 raspberries
3 tablespoons simple syrup (see page 9)
1½ ounces white tequila (or berry-infused tequila; see page 86)
¾ ounce Cointreau
splash of lime juice
additional raspberries, for garnish

Combine the ingredients in a blender with ¾ cup ice. Blend until smooth and pour into a glass. Garnish with whole raspberries.

Blueberry MARGARITA

Using the same recipe as above, substitute ¼ cup fresh blueberries for the raspberries. Garnish with whole blueberries.

Tequila Cobbler

4 to 5 blueberries
1 strawberry
½ lime, cut into quarters
1 orange slice
1 tablespoon sugar
2 ounces white tequila
1 ounce triple sec

Mash together the blueberries, strawberry, lime wedges, and orange slice with the sugar with a spoon. Add the tequila and triple sec and stir. Dump into a cocktail shaker with 1 cup ice and shake vigorously. Pour into a glass.

Lagerita

2 ounces white tequila
1 ounce Cointreau
1 ounce lemon juice
1 ounce simple syrup (see page 9)
2 ounces light beer
lemon wedge, for garnish

Combine the tequila, Cointreau, lemon juice, and simple syrup in a cocktail shaker and shake vigorously. Strain into a pilsner glass or beer mug. Top off with the beer and garnish with a lemon wedge.

White Grape MARGARITA

2 ounces tequila
1 ounce triple sec
1 ounce white grape juice
½ ounce lime juice
6 to 7 whole green grapes
frozen grapes, for garnish

Combine the ingredients in a blender with ¾ cup ice and blend until smooth. Pour into a glass. Garnish with speared frozen grapes.

69

Island MARGARITA

2 ounces tequila
1 ounce triple sec
1 ounce pineapple juice
¾ ounce guava juice
¾ ounce papaya juice
½ ounce lime juice

Combine the ingredients in a cocktail shaker filled with ¾ cup ice and shake vigorously. Pour into a glass.

Caribbean MARGARITA

3 ounces pineapple juice
1½ ounces coconut rum
1 ounce tequila
¾ ounce grenadine
lime wedge and maraschino cherry, for garnish

Combine the ingredients in a cocktail shaker filled with ¾ cup ice and shake vigorously. Pour into a glass. If serving frozen, combine the ingredients in a blender with ¾ cup ice and blend until smooth. Pour into a glass. Garnish with a lime wedge and a maraschino cherry.

Madras

72

A new twist on the classic cocktail, the Madras.

- 3 ounces orange juice
- 1 ounce white tequila
- 1 ounce triple sec
- 1 ounce cranberry juice
- orange wedge, for garnish
- coarse sugar (optional), for garnish

Combine the ingredients in a cocktail shaker filled with ¾ cup ice and shake vigorously. Pour into a glass. Garnish with an orange wedge. For a pink-hued rim, dip the rim of the glass in grenadine before coating with sugar.

MARGARITA *Bay Breeze*

73

Substitute pineapple juice for the orange juice in the recipe above for a twist on the classic cocktail, the Bay Breeze.

Sauvignon MARGARITA

2 ounces tequila
2 ounces Sauvignon Blanc
1 ounce Cointreau
1 ounce lemon juice
1 ounce simple syrup (see page 9)
lemon peel, for garnish

Combine the ingredients in a cocktail shaker filled with ice and shake vigorously. Strain into a wine glass. Garnish with lemon peel.

74

Marga Raider

For a power boost, this margarita is a great alternative to the popular "Red Bull and Vodka."

- **2 ounces tequila**
- **1 ounce triple sec**
- **½ ounce lime juice**
- **½ ounce lemon juice**
- **½ ounce simple syrup (see page 9)**
- **2 ounces carbonated power drink (e.g., Red Bull)**
- **lime wedge, for garnish**

Combine the tequila, triple sec, lime juice, lemon juice, and simple syrup in a cocktail shaker filled with ¾ cup ice and shake vigorously. Pour into a glass. Top off with the power drink and garnish with a lime wedge.

Sangria Rita

1 orange slice
1 lemon slice
1 lime slice
1 tablespoon sugar
3 ounces red wine (inexpensive)
1½ ounces tequila

Mash together the orange, lemon, and lime slices with the sugar
and red wine with a spoon. Add the tequila and ¾ cup ice and
shake vigorously in a cocktail shaker. Pour everything, including
the ice and mashed fruit, into a glass.

76

White Zinfandel
MARGARITA

White Zinfandel, a sweeter wine than Sauvignon Blanc, makes a
pretty pink Margarita. This is a refreshing summer cocktail.

> 3 ounces white zinfandel
> ½ ounce tequila
> ½ ounce lemon juice
> ½ ounce lemon juice
> splash of Cointreau
> coarse sugar (optional), for garnish

Combine the ingredients in a cocktail shaker filled with ice and
shake vigorously. Strain into a glass. Coat the rim of the glass with
coarse sugar, if desired.

77

Sparkling MARGARITA

1 ounce tequila
½ ounce Cointreau
1 ounce lemon juice
1 ounce simple syrup (see page 9)
2 ounces champagne (or sparkling wine)
lemon peel, for garnish

Combine the tequila, Cointreau, lemon juice, and simple syrup in a cocktail shaker and shake vigorously. Strain into a glass. Top off with the champagne and garnish with a lemon peel.

Rain MARGARITA

1½ ounces tequila
1½ ounces white cranberry juice
1 ounce spring water
½ ounce Cointreau
½ ounce sake
1 teaspoon sugar
bamboo stick, for garnish

Combine the ingredients in a cocktail shaker filled with ice and
shake vigorously. Strain into a glass. Garnish with a bamboo stick.

Avocado-Cilantro
MARGARITA

Cilantro adds a subtle, fresh quality to the margarita. It's the perfect accompaniment to chips and guacamole.

2 ounces tequila
1½ ounces simple syrup (see page 9)
1 ounce Grand Marnier
1 ounce lime juice
¼ ripe avocado
1 to 2 tablespoons chopped fresh cilantro
2 to 3 cilantro leaves, for garnish
celery salt (optional), for garnish

Combine the ingredients in a blender with ¾ cup ice and blend until smooth. Pour into a glass. Garnish with cilantro leaves. Coat the rim with a mixture of celery salt and regular coarse salt, if desired.

Asian Pear MARGARITA

1½ ounces white tequila
1 ounce pear brandy (e.g., Poire William)
½ ounce lemon juice
½ ounce simple syrup (see page 9)
¼ Asian pear (with the peel)
pear slice, for garnish

Combine the ingredients in a blender with ¾ cup ice. Blend until smooth. Pour into a glass and garnish with a pear slice.

Sake MARGARITA

1½ ounces plum wine
½ ounce tequila
½ ounce sake
½ ounce lime juice
½ ounce simple syrup (see page 9)
cucumber slice (optional), for garnish

Combine the ingredients in a cocktail shaker filled with ice and
shake vigorously. Strain into a glass. If serving frozen, combine the
ingredients in a blender with ¾ cup ice and blend until smooth.
Pour into a glass. Garnish with a cucumber slice, if desired.

Bamboo MARGARITA

A variation on the Sake Margarita, but a little sweeter.

> 1 ounce white tequila
> 1 ounce simple syrup (see page 9)
> ¾ ounce sake
> ½ ounce Midori
> ½ ounce lemon juice
> ½ ounce lime juice
> bamboo stick (optional), for garnish

Combine the ingredients in a cocktail shaker filled with ¾ cup ice and shake vigorously. Pour into a glass. Garnish with a bamboo stick.

Hot Chile MARGARITA

Tastes just like a regular Margarita, but with a spicy kick.

- 1½ ounces tequila
- 1 ounce triple sec
- 1 ounce simple syrup (see page 9)
- ½ ounce lime juice
- ½ ounce lemon juice
- 3 to 4 dashes of Tabasco hot sauce
- red chile peppers (optional), for garnish

Combine the ingredients in a cocktail shaker filled with ice and shake vigorously. Pour into a glass and serve. Garnish with whole or sliced red chile peppers, if desired.

86

Bloody Rita

4 ounces Bloody Mary Mix
1 ounce tequila
½ ounce lime juice
lime wedge, for garnish

Combine the ingredients in a margarita glass with ¾ cup ice and stir. You can coat the rim with a mixture of celery salt and regular coarse salt. Garnish with a lime wedge.

Golden Cadillac

A twist on a classic: the Golden Cadillac with a Margarita spin.

2 ounces tequila
1½ ounces Galiano
1 ounce simple syrup (see page 9)
½ ounce lime juice
½ ounce lemon juice

Combine the ingredients in a cocktail shaker filled with ice and shake vigorously. Strain into a glass.

Hazelnut MARGARITA

A great dessert margarita for those with a penchant for hazelnut.

> 2 ounces tequila
> 1½ ounces Frangelico (hazelnut liqueur)
> ½ ounce lemon juice
> coarse white sugar or light brown sugar, for garnish

Combine the ingredients in a cocktail shaker filled with ice and shake vigorously. Strain into a glass. If serving frozen, combine the ingredients in a blender with ¾ cup ice and blend until smooth. Pour into a glass. You can coat the rim with white sugar or light brown sugar.

Mulled MARGARITA

A warm version of an old holiday classic.

4 cups apple cider
4 to 5 apple slices (red and/or green apples)
6 whole cloves
4 to 5 dashes cinnamon
1 ounce Grand Marnier
¾ ounce white tequila
4 ounces hot mulled cider
cinnamon stick (optional), for garnish

To make mulled cider, combine the cider, apple slices, cloves, and cinnamon in a pot and heat until boiling. Let boil for about 5 minutes. Ladle the mulled cider into a coffee mug. Add the Grand Marnier and tequila. Garnish with a cinnamon stick, if desired.

Spiced Apple MARGARITA

Vary the recipe above for a cooler Spiced Apple Margarita. Combine 2 ounces mulled cider with 1½ ounces tequila and ¾ ounce Grand Marnier in a cocktail shaker filled with ice. Shake well and strain into a glass. Garnish with a cinnamon stick and an apple slice.

Blonde MARGARITA

2 ounces light cream (or half-and-half)
1 ounce tequila
1 ounce vanilla schnapps
1 ounce simple syrup (see page 9)
simple syrup and superfine sugar, for garnish
vanilla bean (optional), for garnish

Combine the ingredients in a cocktail shaker filled with ice and shake vigorously. Strain into a chilled cocktail glass. For a sugar rim, wet the rim of the chilled glass in simple syrup and dip into superfine sugar several times to ensure coverage. Garnish with vanilla bean, if desired.

Cinnamon MARGARITA

Add ½ ounce cinnamon schnapps to the Blonde Margarita recipe for a spicy finish. Coat the rim in a mixture of sugar and cinnamon.

Old Fashioned

MARGARITA

½ lime, cut into 2 quarters
1 orange slice
2 pitted Bing cherries
1 ounce simple syrup (see page 9)
1½ ounces gold tequila
1 ounce triple sec
2 dashes Angostura bitters (optional)

Mash together the lime quarters, orange slice, Bing cherries, and simple syrup. Add the tequila, triple sec, and bitters, if using, to the mashed fruit. Pour into a cocktail shaker with ¾ cup ice and shake vigorously, for about 20 seconds. Pour into a cocktail glass.

Southern MARGARITA

Substitute Southern Comfort for the triple sec for a spicier, full-bodied margarita.

MARGARITA *du Café*

96

2 ounces chilled espresso
1½ ounces Kahlúa
1 ounce tequila
½ ounce light cream
coffee beans (optional), for garnish

Combine the ingredients in a cocktail shaker filled with ice and shake vigorously. Strain into a glass. Garnish with coffee beans, if desired.

Frozen Mocha-rita

97

Replace the light cream with a scoop of vanilla ice cream and combine the ingredients in a blender with ½ cup ice. Blend until smooth. Garnish with chocolate syrup swirled in the glass.

Cognac MARGARITA

A great after-dinner "cordial" or nightcap.

> 1½ ounces 100% blue agave tequila
> ¾ ounce cognac
> ¾ ounce lemon juice
> ½ ounce simple syrup (see page 9)
> lemon peel, for garnish

Combine the ingredients in a cocktail shaker filled with ice and shake vigorously. Strain into a cognac snifter or Martini glass. Float a lemon peel on top for garnish.

Kentucky 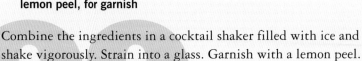 MARGARITA

¾ ounce tequila
¾ ounce bourbon
¾ ounce Cointreau
½ ounce lemon juice
½ ounce orange juice
1 tablespoon honey dissolved in 1 ounce hot water
lemon peel, for garnish

Combine the ingredients in a cocktail shaker filled with ice and shake vigorously. Strain into a glass. Garnish with a lemon peel.

99

Shirley Temple Rita

1 ounce simple syrup (see page 9)
½ ounce lime juice
½ ounce lemon juice
3 ounces Sprite
½ ounce Grenadine (cherry syrup)
maraschino cherry and lime wedge, for garnish
coarse sugar (optional), for garnish

Combine the simple syrup, lime juice, and lemon juice in a cocktail shaker with 1 cup ice and shake vigorously. Pour into a glass. Top off with Sprite. Add grenadine. Garnish with the cherry and lime wedge. If desired, coat the rim of the glass in coarse sugar.

Virgin MARGARITA

2 ounces simple syrup (see page 9)
1 ounce lime juice
1 ounce lemon juice
1 ounce orange juice
lime wedge, for garnish

Combine the ingredients in a cocktail shaker filled with ice and shake vigorously. Pour into a glass. If serving frozen, combine the ingredients in a blender with ¾ cup ice and blend until smooth. Pour into a glass. Garnish with a lime wedge.